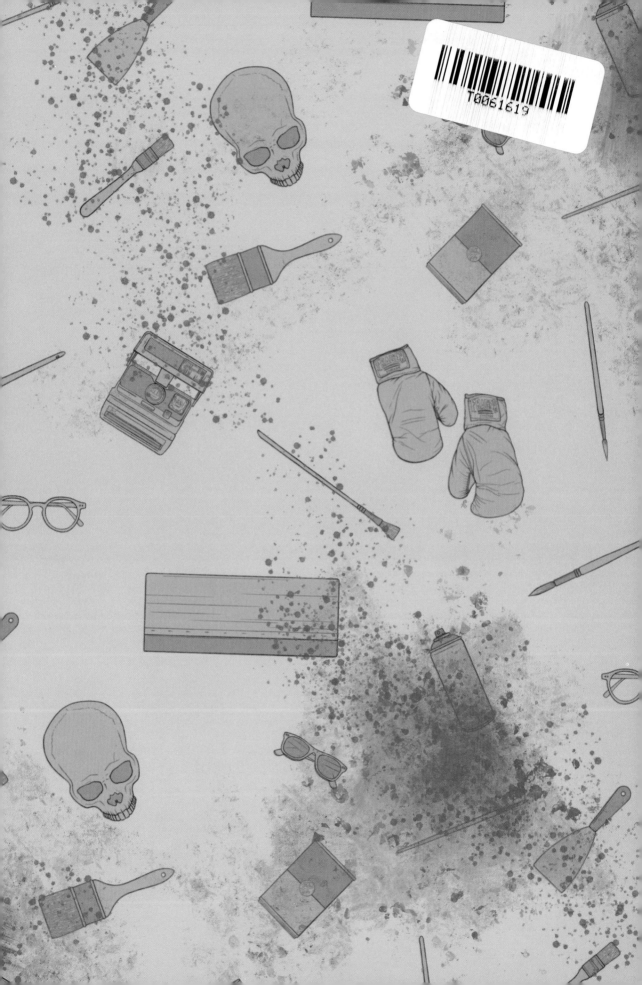

T0061619

Published in 2023 by Orange Mosquito
An Imprint of Welbeck Children's Limited
part of Welbeck Publishing Group.
Based in London and Sydney.
www.welbeckpublishing.com

In collaboration with Mosquito Books Barcelona S.L.

© Mosquito Books Barcelona, SL 2022
Text © Francesca Ferretti de Blonay 2022
Illustration © Carmen Casado 2022
Translation: Laura McGloughlin
Publisher: Margaux Durigon
Production: Jess Brisley

All rights reserved. No part of this publication may be reproduced,
stored in a retrieval system, or transmitted in any form or by any means,
electronically, mechanical, photocopying, recording or otherwise, without
the prior permission of the copyright owners and the publishers

ISBN: 9781914519796
eISBN: 9781914519802

Printed in China
10 9 8 7 6 5 4 3 2 1

FSC
www.fsc.org
MIX
Paper | Supporting
responsible forestry
FSC® C020056

Orange Mosquito, an Imprint of Welbeck encourages diversity and different
viewpoints. However, all views, thoughts, and opinions expressed in this
book are the author's own and are not necessarily representative of Welbeck
Publishing Group as an organisation. All material in this book is set out in
good faith for general guidance and information; Welbeck Publishing Group
makes no representations or warranties of any kind, express or implied, with
respect to the accuracy, completeness, suitability or currency of the contents
of this book, and specifically disclaims, to the extent permitted by law, any
implied warranties of merchantability or fitness for a particular purpose
and any injury, illness, damage, death, liability or loss incurred, directly or
indirectly from the use or application of any of the information contained
in this book.

Francesca Ferretti de Blonay · Bernat Velo

ANDY WARHOL & JEAN-MICHEL BASQUIAT

ORANGE
M·O·S·Q·U·I·T·O

NEW YORK

In New York City, a global beacon of creativity, street art was flourishing, making it an affordable product that more people could buy.

WHERE?

Artists from all over the world congregated in Manhattan's East Village, and it became the artistic center of New York's underground culture.

POP CULTURE

From then on, art was no longer reserved for the elite: now it was for everyone. Art was popularized, even becoming a way of life.

POP ART

Pop art uses images from popular culture (for example, from advertising) to create art. Andy Warhol was a leading figure in this style of art.

STREET ART

All aboard the emotional rollercoaster! A new artistic form of expressing yourself based on improvisation had come about. To a hip-hop beat, graffiti artists like Jean-Michel Basquiat took over the streets.

WHEN?

With over a 30-year age gap between the two artists, Andy Warhol and Jean-Michel Basquiat's paths crossed in the 1980s.

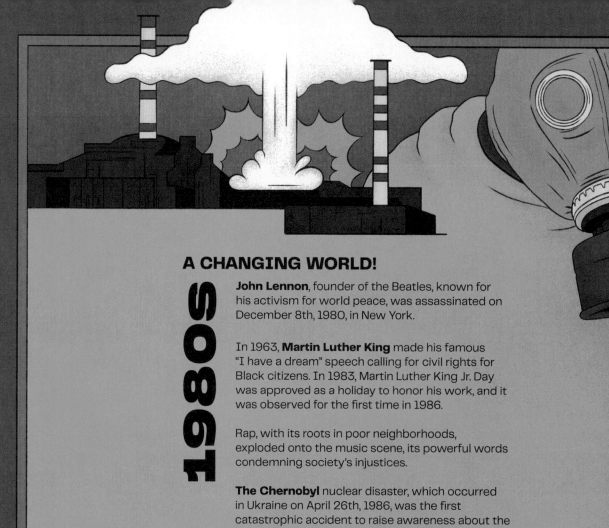

A CHANGING WORLD!

1980S

John Lennon, founder of the Beatles, known for his activism for world peace, was assassinated on December 8th, 1980, in New York.

In 1963, **Martin Luther King** made his famous "I have a dream" speech calling for civil rights for Black citizens. In 1983, Martin Luther King Jr. Day was approved as a holiday to honor his work, and it was observed for the first time in 1986.

Rap, with its roots in poor neighborhoods, exploded onto the music scene, its powerful words condemning society's injustices.

The Chernobyl nuclear disaster, which occurred in Ukraine on April 26th, 1986, was the first catastrophic accident to raise awareness about the need to protect the planet.

Internet became the official name of the global information network. It was invented to strengthen communication between different academic and governmental institutions in the United States.

Macintosh, the first personal computer launched by Apple on January 24th, 1984, was the start of the human–machine dialogue through graphics.

The fall of the **Berlin Wall** in November 1989 meant the end of the Cold War between the Eastern and Western blocs.

The first **Walkman**, a cassette player that allowed the user to listen to music anywhere, was launched in 1979, in Japan.

JEAN-MICHEL

Jean-Michel Basquiat was born on December 22nd, 1960, in Brooklyn, New York. His mother Matilde often took him to museums and this is where his love of art began. He was a precocious child who spent much of his time drawing.

THE ACCIDENT

But one day a tragedy happened. Jean-Michel was knocked down by a car right in front of his house when he was only seven years old! As a result of this accident his arm was badly broken, and he suffered various other injuries. It was during his convalescence that he learned to draw the human body.

SAMO ©

Jean-Michel was a rebellious teenager, so his mother sent him to a school for the exceptionally gifted to try to get him to focus on his artistic abilities. However, at age 18, he left home and began to draw graffiti on the walls of buildings around Manhattan. His graffiti, which he signed with his artist name SAMO, was like a provocative war-cry against the intellectual elite. One year later, Jean-Michel Basquiat, aka SAMO, began to paint.

LIFE IS
CONFUSING AT
THIS. POINT.

-SAMO©

BACKGROUND

Basquiat often painted in Armani suits and barefoot, in an improvised studio within a gallery. Inspiring jazz melodies played as he worked. When he ran out of canvases, he would paint his girlfriend's dresses or the furniture in the house.

ARTISTIC UNIVERSE

After his childhood accident, Jean-Michel developed a strong interest in the human body, and in geniuses like Leonardo da Vinci and Twombly. Composed of symbols, words, and collages, his work provoked intense feelings. His idols, like the boxer Cassius Clay, took pride of place in his art, highlighting the fact that Basquiat had been born in a racist country, something he would never stop condemning.

A STAR IS BORN

Bursting with talent, Basquiat painted, shot films, and played in a jazz band. He was a fascinating artist! His exhibitions were very successful: by the time he finished a painting it was already sold. He left a spectacular life's work of 800 paintings and 1,500 drawings.

THEMES

Basquiat painted everything: postcards, T-shirts, door and window frames, the walls of houses to which he was invited, or whatever he found on the street. He tackled many subjects, through multiple layers, on a single canvas.

He was interested in the history of the African American people and spoke openly about death. For this reason, skeletons, skulls, and details of the human body appear in many of his drawings.

He loved to draw city streets, one of his favorite settings, as well as his Black idols: poets, musicians, and sportsmen, which he drew in postures of victory, as saints with haloes or as crowned kings. He often expressed his discontent and rage at racism and social injustice.

ANDY

Andy Warhol was born on August 4th, 1928, in Forest City, Pennsylvania, the son of Slovakian immigrants. The "American Dream" saw him rise from being a dishwasher to a millionaire. After graduating in Fine Arts, he became a commercial illustrator and moved to St. Mark's Place, New York City, where the street artists of the time were living.

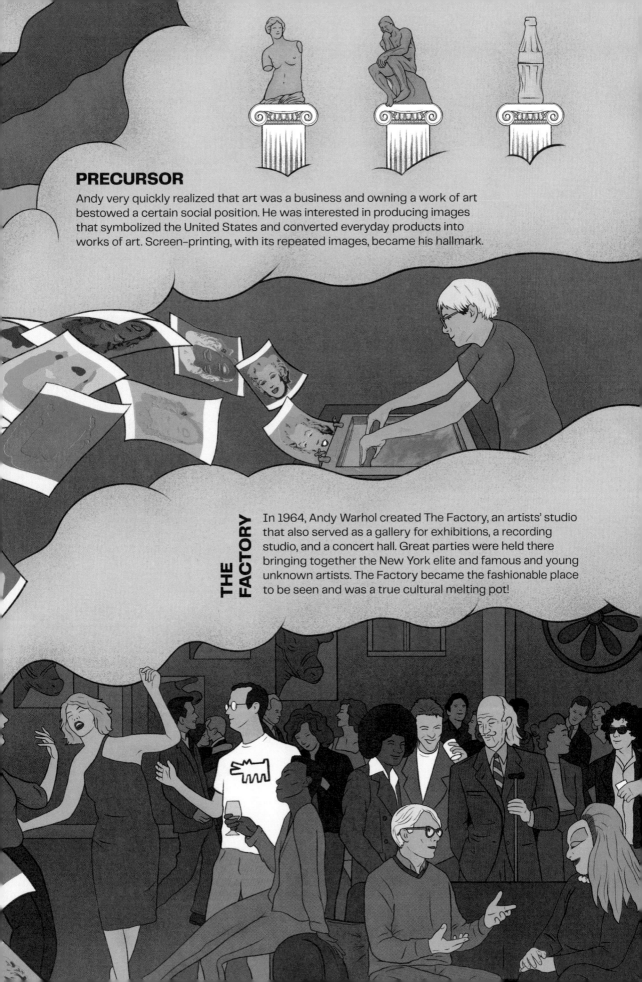

PRECURSOR

Andy very quickly realized that art was a business and owning a work of art bestowed a certain social position. He was interested in producing images that symbolized the United States and converted everyday products into works of art. Screen-printing, with its repeated images, became his hallmark.

THE FACTORY

In 1964, Andy Warhol created The Factory, an artists' studio that also served as a gallery for exhibitions, a recording studio, and a concert hall. Great parties were held there bringing together the New York elite and famous and young unknown artists. The Factory became the fashionable place to be seen and was a true cultural melting pot!

BACKGROUND

In The Factory, at 33 Union Square, Andy would walk around with his Polaroid camera slung around his neck, snapping photographs. He would swap around his latest prints while bands, like The Velvet Underground, were rehearsing for their next concert. Andy would be producing a chain of screen prints while at his side his assistants would be organizing his next exhibition. The Factory was a hive of creativity!

UNIVERSE

Andy's heart was torn between art and advertising! While creating ads for *Vogue* and *Harper's Bazaar* magazines, he also reproduced original drawings on blotting paper and transferred the lines in charcoal onto another page. His posters of repeated motifs in bright colors were a huge success.

STAR SYSTEM

The enigmatic Warhol liked to attend the fashionable New York social events where he could mix with the rich and famous. He was attracted by iconic celebrities with tragic endings, like Marilyn Monroe and Mao Tse-tung. He made brightly colored portraits of them, and it was these that made him famous.

THEMES

In the 1960s, Andy Warhol began to photograph famous people, as well as American consumer products of the era, like Coca-Cola or Campbell's soup. Marilyn Monroe, Campbell's cans, Mick Jagger ... these, to name a few, became symbols that described American society.

The everyday products that people bought were transformed into genuine works of art. Playing with repetition, Andy would reproduce objects or portraits on the same canvas. He was an artist and great professional who knew how to go beyond the material he worked with to create fantasy.

INTRODUCTION

Eighteen-year-old Basquiat was selling postcards on the street when he saw Andy Warhol in a Soho restaurant. He went in and offered him one of his postcards for a dollar. Amused, Andy bought it, and then his agent threw the boy out. It was one of the happiest days of the young artist's life.

FIRST CONTACT

Basquiat and Warhol officially met years later. They met for lunch and Andy's friend took a photo of the two artists together with Andy's Polaroid. Jean-Michel grabbed the photo and went back to his studio. A few hours later, Basquiat's agent returned with a freshly painted 5-foot canvas of Basquiat next to Andy. Warhol was captivated by the young artist's talent!

DOUBLE-DEALING

The two artists were at different stages in their lives. Warhol was a renowned star seeking a fresh stimulus and Basquiat a rising name from the American underground scene who was looking for support in the contemporary art circle. They were destined to meet each other!

PERFECT UNDERSTANDING

Basquiat and Warhol would go for walks together, visit exhibitions, and frequent the same clubs. They enjoyed learning about each other's lives. At that time, Jean–Michel Basquiat was participating in numerous projects with other artists. He was successful and earning money. Despite this, he felt alone and in Warhol he found a confidante, even a soulmate! Although there were more than 30 years between them, their connection was genuine. They shared a great complicity, personally as well as artistically.

COLLABORATION

Between 1984 and 1985, the two artists collaborated in the creation of a series of works that combined their two styles. They took turns to paint on the same canvas, each adding to or changing elements of the picture. An improvised dialogue was underway. The result was a multi-layered joint work, in which the exchange between two generations revealed a respectful kind of father–son rivalry.

100 CANVASES WITH FOUR HANDS

The two artists gave a lot to each other. They were able to share and utilize their different artistic styles to work together. Thanks to Basquiat, Warhol started painting again. As for Basquiat, he learned a lot about the technique of screen printing. Together they formed a great duo who created more than 100 canvases with their four hands.

A SEDUCTIVE PAIR OF UNDERGROUND ARTISTS

The collaboration of the two artists made headlines. In 1985, they exhibited their paintings in various galleries in New York, Zurich, and Tokyo. Unfortunately, the success of the two geniuses of pop art and street art wasn't as great as had been expected.

THE REACTION OF THE PRESS

Even though theirs was an original collaboration, the press showed no mercy to the two artists: Warhol was accused of manipulating Basquiat, and Basquiat of letting himself go. Their artistic relationship was a scandal! A devastating article put an end to their joint work, but not to their mutual admiration.

SEPARATION AND END

The verdict of the cultural media was definitive: the four-handed work wasn't as valuable as what each artist could produce on their own. Warhol and Basquiat set out on their artistic paths alone once again.

Andy Warhol continued with his work as an observer of the trends of the era, until he unexpectedly died after gallbladder surgery on February 22nd, 1987.

For his part, Basquiat was going through a rough patch. His girlfriend had left him, and the news of Warhol's death plunged him into a deep depression.

He never recovered from the death of his friend. In 1987, he created the painting *Gravestone* in honor of Andy Warhol.

After a course of rehabilitation in Hawaii, Basquiat returned to New York where he quickly went back to his old ways. Finally, on August 12th, 1988, Basquiat was found lifeless in his apartment. He was only 27 years old!

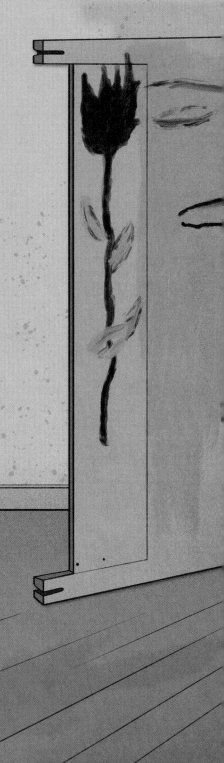

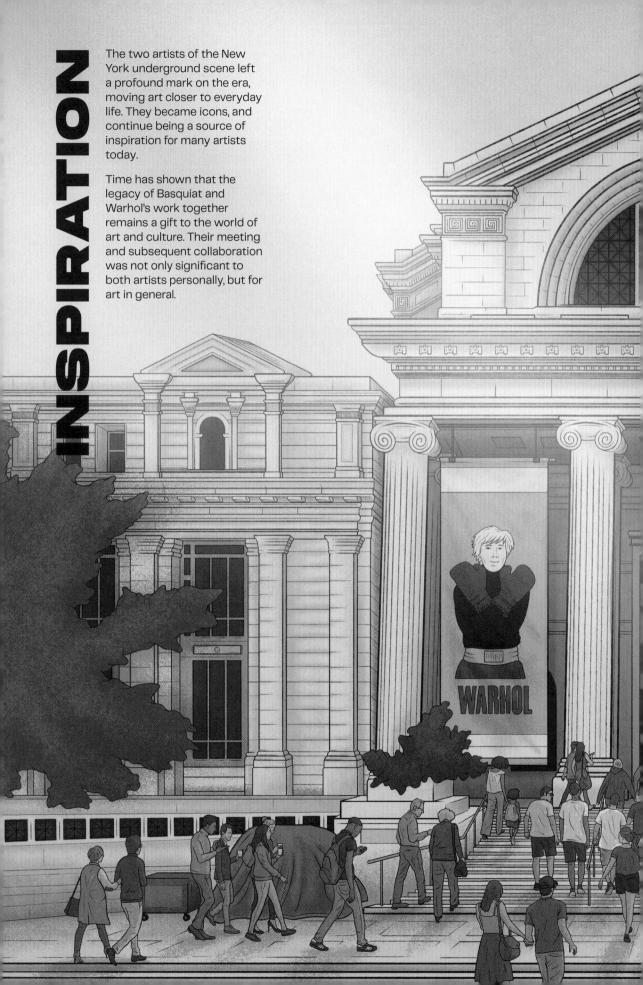

INSPIRATION

The two artists of the New York underground scene left a profound mark on the era, moving art closer to everyday life. They became icons, and continue being a source of inspiration for many artists today.

Time has shown that the legacy of Basquiat and Warhol's work together remains a gift to the world of art and culture. Their meeting and subsequent collaboration was not only significant to both artists personally, but for art in general.

WARHOL

FAME

After both of their untimely deaths, it wasn't long before the world of art was talking about Basquiat and Warhol again. Their collaboration is remembered in every book about art. Whenever one of them is mentioned, so too is the other. Their work has been shown in modern and contemporary art museums all over the world: Bilbao, New York, Pittsburgh, Paris, Milan, and Haiti. And many designers and stylists have fun representing Basquiat and Warhol's work on objects and clothes, such as a chair, a T-shirt, or even a pair of pants.

BASQUIAT

**FAMOUS
QUOTES**

Jean-Michel Basquiat

I don't think about art when I'm working.
I try to think about life.

The Black person is the protagonist in most of my paintings.
I realized that I didn't see many paintings with Black people
in them.

I never know how really to describe it except maybe,
I don't know, I don't know how to describe my work,
because it's not always the same thing.

I am not a black artist, I am an artist.

I wanted to be a star, not a gallery mascot.

Happiness will find you when you stop hiding.

Good business is the best art.

Publicity is like eating peanuts.
Once you start you can't stop.

America started the tradition where the richest consumers buy
essentially the same things as the poorest.

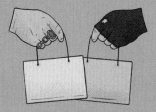

When you think about it, department stores are kind
of like museums.

Art is already advertising. The *Mona Lisa* could have been used as a
support for a chocolate brand, Coca–Cola or anything else.

FAMOUS
QUOTES

Andy Warhol

SKULL

A WORK BY BASQUIAT

Basquiat was twenty years old when he painted *Skull*.

Basquiat had a passion for anatomy, and this can be seen in the complex universe hidden within the image of the skull, and the artistic game playing out between the inside and outside of the head. The jaw is that of a skull, but the face has eyes, a nose, and ears and the top of the head is covered in hair. Black skin covers the right side of the head. The corner of the mouth is curved, the eyes bulging, and the teeth clenched. The decomposing head has cuts and scars, which perhaps reveal the deep anguish that Basquiat experienced in his short life.

Skull is an emotionally moving piece of art, and the image retains much of its mystery.

Themes: death, life, pain, the condition of Black people, the artist's place in society, the human being in all its dimensions.

Technique: acrylic paint, with touches of pencil here and there which create precise strokes and allow for detailed drawing.

CAMPBELL'S SOUP CANS

A WORK BY WARHOL

In 1962, Andy Warhol created a piece of work made up of 32 posters all showing the same thing: a Campbell's brand soup can. The 32 posters were shown at a New York art gallery. It was a very high-profile event! The piece was the first of its kind in the United States, where pop art was still unknown.

The serigraphs, which at first glance seemed identical, were actually different and every soup had a different flavor, from clam chowder and chicken noodle through to beef noodle and vegetable.

Curious anecdote: Andy Warhol told everyone he ate a can of Campbell's soup every day. A very clever advertising trick!

Themes: the consumer society, the American way of life, childhood, the brand that becomes a symbol and a work of art.

Technique: screen printing in which the product is painted by hand. The motif is reproduced through screen printing and serially repeated, then repeated in a series of various colors.

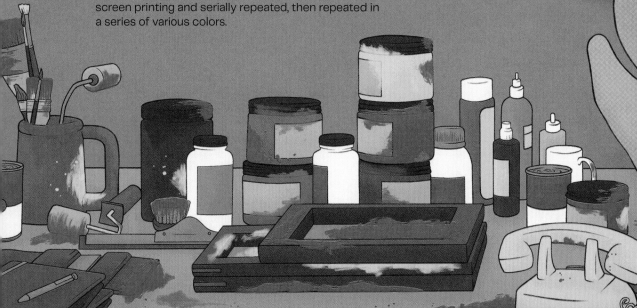

AL DÍAZ
Puerto Rican artist and co-creator of SAMO with Basquiat. The two graffiti artists filled the streets of Manhattan with poetic messages and protests. Al Díaz is still a graffiti artist.

MADONNA
Friend of Jean-Michel Basquiat, Madonna arrived in New York at the end of the 1970s, to be a dancer. There she signed her first contract with a record company and began her career as a singer.

KEITH HARING
American artist, illustrator, and sculptor based in New York's East Village, where he discovered the underground culture of the 1980s. He was a friend of Madonna and Jean-Michel Basquiat, with whom he exhibited his work.

ARTISTS AND FRIENDS

GERARD MALANGA

Poet and photographer, Malanga was Andy Warhol's main assistant from the 1960s. With him he founded the magazine Interview in 1969, as well as making various films like *Divan*, *Vinyl*, and *Chelsea Girls*.

GRACE JONES

Born in Jamaica, this singer, songwriter, and model moved with her parents to New York and then Paris where she became a fashion icon. It was there that she met Andy Warhol and became his muse.

GLOSSARY

Advertising: a mean of giving information to the public about a product, a service or an event, in order to attract interest and generate sales.

Anatomy: the study of the different body parts of living things.

Cassius Clay: an American professional boxer and activist. He is also known as Muhammad Ali, as he changed his name in 1964 when he converted to the religion of Islam.

Graffiti: a text, mark or drawing made in a public space.

Leonardo da Vinci: an Italian artist, mathematician, scientist and inventor. Two of his most famous paintings are the Mona Lisa and The Last Supper. He designed early versions of the helicopter and parachute.

Mao Tse-tung: a Chinese ruler from 1949 to 1976, who led China's Communist party. His name is also spelled in the Latin-alphabet as Mao Zedong.

Marilyn Monroe: an American actress, model and singer. Her birth name was Norma Jean. She was a supporter of civil rights and became the second woman in U.S. history to own her own production company.

Pop Art: a style of art based on bold images of everyday objects or symbols. It is the combination of fine art with popular culture.

Screen printing: a printing technique where ink is pressed trough a stencilled mesh to create a pattern or design.

Twombly: an American artist who used the nickname 'Cy', known for his large-scale, scribble and calligraphic-style graffiti paintings.

Underground culture: Counterculture, which goes against the dominant culture.